IMAGES OF ENGLAND

ILFRACOMBE

Ilfracombe Potens Salubritate – Ilfracombe Strong for Health. The coat of arms, adopted in 1894, incorporates the family arms of the Bourchier Wreys, the Lords of the Manor, with dolphins, battle-axes and water containers, symbolizing the water they carried on the Crusades. The six ships signify the ones Ilfracombe provided for the siege of Calais, and the waves and oar represent the Local Board of Health, which became the Urban District Council.

IMAGES OF ENGLAND

ILFRACOMBE

SUE PULLEN AND JANE HARDING

WILDERSMOUTH, ILFRACOMBE.

Charles Kingsley and John Betjeman both wrote in praise of the natural beauty they found in Ilfracombe.

First published in 2003 by Tempus Publishing

Reprinted in 2010 by
The History Press
The Mill, Brimscombe Port,
Stroud, Gloucestershire, GL5 2QG
www.thehistorypress.co.uk

Reprinted in 2011

British Library Cataloguing in Publication Data.
A catalogue record for this book is available from the British Library.

ISBN 978 0 7524 2538 2

Typesetting and origination by Tempus Publishing.
Printed and bound in Great Britain by
Marston Book Services Limited, Didcot

Contents

The first glimpse of buildings around the edge of Ilfracombe harbour, taken from the ancient stone pier in the late nineteenth century.

Acknowledgements

The authors, who are managers at Ilfracombe Museum, would like to thank the staff and volunteers, and their partners, for their patience during the time spent gathering the photographs and information together. We would like to dedicate the book to Reuben Harvey, who could date pictures with such interesting accuracy, but who sadly passed away before this book was published.

The illustrations are reproduced with the kind permission of the Ilfracombe Museum Trustees; Foto Keith Powell Photography – Ilfracombe: Pier view p.28; Peter Robins: coconut oil p.101, eggs p.126; Arthur Street: Picture Hall p.107.

Introduction

'Dear Old Ilfracombe by the Sea', so begins the local song published in 1905 which reflects the thoughts of millions of holidaymakers and day-trippers who have visited this unique seaside town.

The earliest known inhabitants were responsible for a Bronze Age burial chamber that was uncovered on Hillsborough (Heles Burrow) in 1934, when a stop trench was being dug during a gorse fire. The earthworks of a later Iron Age hill fort are visible on Hillsborough today.

The Domesday survey calls the area Alfriencoma – 'combe of the sons of Alfred'. No one is quite sure who he was as there are no written records about the Saxon inhabitants. After the Norman Conquest, William of Normandy acquired vast amounts of Devon and sublet them. Alfriencoma went to a Robert, whose manor consisted of twelve villeins, twelve smallholders and five slaves and their families. These forebears recognised their home as a safe harbour and landing place and built their first ships.

The port is mentioned on many occasions as a gathering point for troops en route to Spain, France and Ireland. A well-known reference says that in 1345 Ilfracombe furnished King Edward III with either eighty-two or ninety-six sailors and six ships, Liverpool providing only one vessel with five men, indicating how important Ilfracombe was as a port. The ships then would have resembled a small *Mary Rose* with a fighting castle fore and aft, one mast, and ten or twelve men rowing. Weapons consisted of longbows and crossbows, as there were no cannons, and with no compass, navigation by day made it necessary to keep the coast in sight, headlands being important route marks.

Ilfracombe harbour is a deep rock-bound indent and it would have needed little alteration to make it a sheltered haven. Though too small for many of today's trading ships, its situation as the only port on a long stretch of dangerous coast was ideal for the smaller ships of earlier days. The rise and fall of the tides here in the Bristol Channel, once known as the Severn Sea, are among the highest in the world. Trade by sea was preferable as inland bridle paths were suitable only for packhorses and travellers on foot. An early 1800s writer says, 'the coast is by far the most magnificent and picturesque of which Devon can boast but it is only accessible by the worst roads in the kingdom'. Towards the end of that century the roads were improved, steamers gave a regular service and the railway had arrived.

Previous writers and illustrators have hinted that a castle was first built in Tudor times for the protection of shipping in the harbour. During the Civil War, on the 20 August 1644, Royalist leader Sir Francis Doddington attacked Ilfracombe, which had generally taken Parliament's side. He entered from Combe Martin 'passing the castle'; maybe this was the site of Castle House at the bottom of Castle Hill. Twenty-seven houses were reported burnt and eleven defenders died before townsmen and sailors saw off the invaders. Weeks later, the castle commander committed an act of treachery and the fortification fell to Royalists, who seized 'twenty pieces of ordnance, two hundred arms and many barrels of gunpowder'. By April of the following year it had been stormed again, this time by Colonel Sheffield, a Parliamentarian, and from then on Ilfracombe took no further part in the war.

In 1796, during the Napoleonic wars, a six hundred-ton troop ship, the *London*, returning from St Lucia and bound for Bristol, was wrecked in a storm on Rapparee. Numerous stories have been told about this ship and others that were lost here with valuable coin and bullion cargos. A year later, at least three French vessels ventured close to the port and scuttled some local shipping. Legend has it that local women, lead by Betsy Gammon, draped their red flannel petticoats around their shoulders and, carrying broomsticks, imitated the presence of soldiers defending the town. The French turned and headed for Wales where a similar story survives!

During the Victorian age, visitors came to admire the scenery and breathe the pure air. Ilfracombe strived to attract the upper classes that stayed for the whole season with their entire family and personal servants. Magnificent hotels and villas were built, while theatres, halls and public rooms opened to provide entertainment. Transport of a wide variety and quality was available to escort the visitor to the well-stocked shops or adjacent villages. The town's own newspapers, the *Ilfracombe Chronicle* and the *Ilfracombe Gazette and Observer*, apart from listing all those arriving, gave details of postal arrangements, banks, baths, four surgeons, three dentists, the town crier, constable and gas works.

Fear gripped the whole country in 1848 when cholera broke out and it was realised water and sanitary arrangements were to blame. Locally all efforts were made to improve the situation until it became possible to advertise Ilfracombe as the 'healthiest of watering places'.

Many writers and artists have been inspired by their visits to Ilfracombe. Among the most notable are J.M.W. Turner who painted a wild and stormy scene off Ilfracombe, and Albert Goodwin, a Victorian water-colourist. George Eliot wrote her first novel soon after her stay with Henry Lewes in May 1856, at Runnymede Villa. Henry Williamson, author of *Tarka the Otter*, lived in the town during his latter years. Charles Kingsley preached at Holy Trinity Parish Church in 1854 whilst writing *Westward Ho!* He thought that 'There is no pleasanter or cheaper place of cure (to indulge in a puff honest and true) than Ilfracombe, with its quiet nature, and its quiet luxury, its rock fairyland and its sea walks, its downs and combes, its kind people, and if possible, its still kinder climate.'

The Boer War and the World Wars took their toll on Ilfracombe families. There are graphic details of their struggles in the newspapers, but between the wars the town prospered. With the increase in private cars, and changes in visitor expectations and foreign holidays becoming more popular, fortunes fluctuated but the natural beauty endures and Ilfracombe is still a favourite destination for many to visit and live in today.

One

Harbour Life

For centuries families lived, worked and prayed around the inner harbour, a natural safe shelter for their boats and the main point of entry for friend or foe. The ketch *Kate*, seen on the right, sank off Lundy in heavy seas in May 1896, after having discharged her cargo of building materials for the construction of Lundy Island church.

This view from Hillsborough before 1867, shows the harbour area with St Nicholas' Chapel to the right, St Philip and St James' Church in the centre, and to the right of this the second Wesleyan Chapel. The stone pier is thought to have been built in the fourteenth century. An Act of Parliament in 1727 enforced the Lord of the Manor to partly rebuild and lengthen it in 1730.

A print by J. Powell, published in 1830 by H.F. Wildman of Barnstaple is an artistic view of Warp Point. Warpage was a tax levied for the use of the harbour towboats and heavy warp (rope) was kept at the Warp House to help large vessels swing round into the narrow entrance of the harbour.

Evidence of the ship-building industry that was carried out on the south side of the harbour is clearly revealed in the Day & Haghe lithograph published by F. Lammas of Ilfracombe, *c.* 1840. There are no definite records until 1735 when the *Edward* (sixty tons) was constructed. After this many of the larger ships, such as the *Duchess of Clarence* (174 tons) built by William Huxtable, and the *Coronella* (over 300 tons) by Charles Dennis, made voyages to the East Indies, China and South America. One Captain James Bale sailed twenty-two times around Cape Horn. The smart terraces above the harbour were started around 1820.

Fishing was always an important trade and fish a staple diet for local families. When back in port, nets needed mending and the decks scrubbed. It was an arduous job, started young and for life, often in a family business. Mr Alfred Langston photographed this trawler in July 1892.

There are many newspaper reports in the early 1900s of sharks becoming entangled in fishermen's nets and causing a great deal of damage. George Rudd, seen on the left, caught this specimen in 1906. Once a fifteen-foot thresher actually 'jumped' on board the *Alarm* and the passengers had to transfer to another boat while John Williams brought the shark ashore.

At one time the town crier would announce 'Coombe errins, Coombe errins' at the Quay and people would rush down to purchase some. Then hawking became favourable and carts like this one drawn by Tintack the donkey in 1920, would be seen. From left to right: Bill Irwin, Jan (Corky) Bushen, Bob Ralph, Jan Conibear, Ernie Ralph.

Boats in harbour would be repaired, scraped and repainted between tides when the weather was good. The Bethel in the background was established in the early nineteenth century to provide a shelter in all weathers for sailors to rest in safety and comfort. It was open from 5 a.m. to 9 p.m. in the herring season and the attendant was paid £30 per year.

This amazing display of conger and skate was caught off Ilfracombe on 26 November 1906. F. Tuck, A.H. Ewens and boatman N. Barbeary had only been fishing for three hours!

Herrings could be caught in many thousands by boats like the *Rowena*, seen here in 1925, and prices would change almost daily depending on the catch. Some liked them boiled in milk and others baked them in vinegar in the oven. Some were laid down in barrels of salt for the winter or smoked on premises on the Strand and Fore Street.

Wooden ketches moored in the inner harbour were a common sight in the late nineteenth century. They were sturdy vessels used for trading in the Bristol Channel, carrying a variety of bulk cargo such as coal. To keep operating costs down, they could be managed with a small crew, often as a family concern.

A Swedish ship is seen off-loading its cargo of timber at the stone pier in the 1890s. Custom officers, known as 'tide waiters', would check the loading and discharging of cargoes so that necessary fees were paid. Sometimes the town seemed to be full of many different nationalities as vessels sought shelter in stormy weather.

Limestone was brought from Wales in ketches and discharged directly onto the beach at Larkstone, as shown here in the 1870s. Layers of limestone and culm (coal dust) were burnt in the limekiln, part of which can still be seen at the top of the beach. Lime was used for house-building and farmers spread it on their acid soil.

Cattle from Ireland were unloaded with the help of Ilfracombe men using sacking and tackle in 1892. Sometimes beasts would be hoisted overboard to swim ashore, and locals locked their doors as the bulls were wild and caused damage. A report suggested one elderly lady died on the spot when she heard the bellowing at her door.

Horses and donkeys with baskets slung across their backs, sometimes pulling a cart, carried coal up through the cobbled streets from the harbour. These patient creatures were looked after to varying degrees and those less fortunate were half starved and had sores full of coal dust. A caring vicar's wife regularly brought oats on a Sunday to their stables.

'Admiral Rodney set sail from Plymouth on his last and most glorious expedition in 1782' so D. Warrell-Bowring tells us in the book *Ilfracombe Through the Ages*. He captured a French ship off the West Indies but while returning with his prize of gold and silver was shipwrecked on rocks near Rapparee. The pub in Rodney Lane named after him was demolished in 1908.

The Brinkworth and Tanner Gloucester pilot boat seen moored next to a brigantine, was one of many using Ilfracombe as a base over the years. Others included Barry, Newport, Cardiff and Bristol. A number of local men were involved in this tough and dangerous life. Fisher and Williams were reported drowned in March 1899.

A new lifeboat, the *Co-operator No. 2*, given to Ilfracombe by the Co-operative Society, was named and launched on 18 June 1886 'amidst much enthusiasm' by the large number of people on the Quay. Naval Artillery Volunteers manning the rigging on the gunboat Tay gave loud cheers for the boat and her crew.

The Manor House, situated centre behind the houses on the Cove, was built in the early 1700s. The last Lord of the Manor, Sir Bourchier Palk Wrey, came to live here in around 1870 when his daughter moved into Tawstock Court, Barnstaple, after her marriage to Edward Weld of Lulworth Castle. The Dead House at the harbour's edge was used to lay out the bodies of anyone who had died at sea. The buildings on the skyline, from left to right, are The Cliffe Hydro, Castle House and Coronation Terrace and the whole scene is before 1911 when the new sea wall was constructed.

The clockmaker's workshop down on the Cove disappeared soon after this picture was taken in 1911 when the harbour improvements were completed. Elias Hobbs gained considerable notoriety throughout North Devon for his grandfather clocks 'of distinctly his own make'. He died in 1845 and was buried at the Parish Church.

Known as 'The House on Stilts', No. 6 The Strand was demolished in 1935. Architect Allen Hussell was able to look around at that time and described the old oak ship timbers and the peat blocks used between the floors for noise insulation. There were interesting doors with slide openings to look out for the press gang or revenue men and an escape route at the back of the building.

The Chapel on Lantern Hill is dedicated to St Nicholas the patron saint of sailors. It has been a lighthouse since at least 1522 when it was mentioned in a bishops register 'that whoever made a pilgrimage there and kept the light bright would receive an indulgence (the remission of punishment in purgatory) for forty days. The Chapel was used as a reading room for the public during the summer where 'gentlemen amused themselves reading the newspapers and the ladies by scribbling in a scrap book kept for the purpose'. It has also been a home for a family with thirteen children, a laundry and a band practice room.

This Ilfracombe harbour lithograph by L. Haghe, published by Wildman of Barnstaple in around 1830, suggests a tranquil and peaceful setting of sailing days, which belied the reality of the hardships of fishermen and traders and the day-to-day lives of people living in the harbour area.

A turmoil of sea and sky
That rais'd the waves to mountains high
And woke in hearts a shudd'ring
For periled lives this fearful night.

Two

Arriving by Sea

The first steam packets started to arrive in Ilfracombe from 1823, and a regular service up and down the Bristol Channel and across to Swansea developed. The difficulties facing passengers can be seen as they embark on the *Velindra* from Warp House Point in 1870. Often they had to be taken to and from the stone pier in small boats.

A much-needed wooden promenade pier was opened on 16 May 1873 to allow the pleasure steamers to berth and to land the ever-increasing visitors at all stages of the tide. According to the *Ilfracombe Chronicle* the town enjoyed a 'thorough day of rejoicing' with processions, flags, bands and speeches.

The *Alexandra*, *Waverley*, *Lorna Doone* and the *Earl of Dunraven* are shown at the new pier in 1892. On Monday 23 June 1894 it was reported that over 2,500 persons arrived by steamer on no less than seven boats. Trips ran all through the summer and they were advertised as 'commodious and well-appointed vessels with an excellent reputation for speed and comfort'.

The steam packet *Velindra* (1860-1897) was one of the early vessels giving a regular service in the Bristol Channel. She would carry a miscellaneous collection of live and dead stock, merchandise and men to take up work across 'the herring pond'. A blow on the whistle indicated all was loaded and ready to go.

Captain William Pockett, seen here with the staff of the *Velindra*, owned the Bristol Channel Steam Packet Company. He was described as a 'smart and skilful seaman with a generous nature'. He died in 1890 and his business was sold but the name remained. The *Velindra* was advertised in 1894 as the only excursion steamer in the Bristol Channel classed 'A1' at Lloyds.

The *Waverley*, arriving at Ilfracombe around 1890, was a frequent visitor since 1887 when her owners Messrs P. and A. Campbell brought her to Bristol from the Clyde as their first pleasure steamer to work the Bristol Channel. During the First World War she was used for minesweeping and patrolling duties near Ilfracombe and also in the Thames Estuary. Her condition deteriorated to such an extent that she could no longer carry passengers and another of the White Funnel Fleet, the *Barry*, was renamed the *Waverley* in 1919. She continued bringing day-trippers in their thousands which increased the prosperity of the town after the war years. This ship was later sunk off Sunderland during the Second World War. The present *Waverley* was built in 1946 as a replacement for another *Waverley*, which sunk at Dunkirk. She is the last sea-going paddle steamer in the world and a glimpse of an era long past.

Happy day-trippers from South Wales disembark onto the landing stages in 1934. Pictures taken by local photographers of all the new arrivals were made available in postcard form on the same day for visitors to buy as a souvenir of their trip.

Gathered in front of the lifeboat house are the Ilfracombe harbour staff, c. 1910. Fourth from the left, front row, is John Galliver, a pier tollgate attendant; next to him in the boater hat is Councillor Woodward, then harbour master Captain Birmingham who served for fourteen years on the Cape Horn trade ships, then Jack Wilson steamroller driver. By the 1930s, Galliver and Wilson had each worked on the pier for over forty years.

Deterioration of the pier due to storms and part demolition for anti-invasion precautions in 1940 meant that major works had to be carried out. The new pier was opened on 6 July 1952. The timber was replaced with a reinforced concrete structure and more space was provided for car parking.

The men who built the pier, never exceeding twenty-five, were praised by Mr F. Reed, Chairman of Ilfracombe Harbour Committee, saying 'they had worked under conditions that would have tried the hardest of men'. They included from left to right, back row: Fred Leigh, Fred Draper, Jack Nicholls, Bill Quinn, Fred Redmore. Front row: Charlie Schiller, Dick Thomas, Les 'Sausage' Lewis.

Three

Where Shall We Stay?

As expressed in this postcard from around 1914, holidaymakers having 'just arrived at Ilfracombe' by sea, road or railway, had plenty to look forward to. There was an amazing variety of accommodation from which to choose, ranging from the salubrious to the basic in almost every part of town.

ILFRACOMBE HOTEL.

"Believe me, sir, the finest scenery in the world is improved by a good Hotel in the foreground."

THE ILFRACOMBE HOTEL,

Stands in its own Ornamental Grounds, of five acres extending to the SEA BEACH, and a Private Terrace on the north side affords the finest MARINE PROMENADE attached to any hotel in the United Kingdom. The newly-constructed walks overlook the bright clear blue water of the Bristol Channel, and command extensive views of beautiful COAST SCENERY.

The Building has been enlarged for the season 1871, and now contains more than 230 Apartments,—Table d'Hôte and Coffee Rooms, Reading Room, Drawing Room, several suites of Sitting Rooms and Bedrooms, nearly all with Sea View; also large Billiard Room (two Tables), Smoking Room, Baths, &c.

The CUISINE is excellent, the WINES choice, and the appointments throughout perfect.

Good Stabling and Lock-up Coach Houses. Post Horses and Carriages always ready. Sailing Boats and Yachts also provided.

Bedroom, Board and attendance, with use of Public Rooms, from 3½ guineas per week, according to situation of Bedroom. Table d'Hôte daily.

Address—J. BOHN, Ilfracombe, North Devon.

Public Conveyances to and from the Barnstaple Station, on London & South Western Railway. In Summer, daily Service and through Booking from the principal Stations on Great Western, Midland, Bristol and Exeter Railways, *via* Portishead; and a regular Service of Steamers between Bristol, Cardiff, Swansea, Tenby, and Ilfracombe.—See Time Tables.

The Ilfracombe Hotel, as advertised in *The Hand Book of North Devon*, first opened on 22 May 1867. Described as a 'sumptuous monster hotel', it helped to make Ilfracombe a fashionable seaside resort. Amidst great scepticism, the Ilfracombe Hotel and Esplanade Company had been set up in 1863 to embark on this ambitious building project in anticipation of the coming of the railway.

Set in its own grounds on an ideal site on the seashore off Wilder Road where the Landmark Theatre now stands, the Ilfracombe Hotel boasted ornamental grounds of five acres and eight lawn tennis courts. Many important dignitaries visited including Prince Albrect of Prussia who stayed for one month in April 1895.

Mr John White, seen on the right, was well known as the coachman of the Ilfracombe Hotel for many years. Initially a four-horse carriage, then later an omnibus, was used to meet guests from the railway station. The hotel had an enormous staff to cater for the needs of its visitors. In 1886, the three kitchens alone employed about seventy men and women in the season.

The magnificent new lounge hall of the Ilfracombe Hotel was completed in June 1893 at the cost of several hundred pounds. The jardinière in the centre contained a six-foot high palm. Italian and Austrian workmen laid a mosaic and parquet floor. Barum ware on the pedestals were filled with exotic flowers and each alcove was lit with oriental carved brass lamps.

Guests could walk directly onto the hotel's 'beautiful' esplanade. This led down to the seawater swimming baths, which it boasted as was one of the largest in England. Note the absence of the Granville Hotel, which was built high above the Ilfracombe Hotel in 1891.

Overlooking the harbour and adjacent to the quay is one of Ilfracombe's oldest established hostelries, the Royal Britannia, dating back to the eighteenth century. It acquired its royal title when the young Prince of Wales, the future Edward VII, stayed there briefly. For some years, a pony named Bobby was pointed out as the one His Royal Highness rode at Ilfracombe. It is traditionally believed that Nelson stayed here, but there is no documentary evidence for this. In 1867 it was decorated and 'furnished with every accommodation for the comfort of strangers' because of business connections with the newly-built Ilfracombe Hotel. Its proximity to the harbour has always made it a popular choice for guests with a nautical tendency.

The Collingwood Hotel was formerly a terrace of four houses but in this picture of 1897 a new front has been built. The terraces, from left to right, Rupertswood, Coronation and Montpelier, commanded magnificent sea views and had 'every accommodation necessary for residents and visitors'. A public assembly room in the middle of Coronation Terrace provided reading and billiard rooms and a ballroom.

The Esplanade, Moonta and Dudley boarding houses in Capstone Crescent, built in 1893, had a private flight of steps leading to the beach. The uninterrupted sea views gave guests a full sight of excursion steamers passing close by.

The Imperial and the Waverley Hotels, decorated in great style with flags and bunting, were celebrating Queen Victoria's Diamond Jubilee in 1897. The Imperial, in a unique situation facing the sea and Capstone, contained 100 apartments, large coffee and dining rooms, writing, reading and smoking rooms. By 1915 it had electric light, a passenger lift and rooms costing from 2 to $3\frac{1}{2}$ guineas.

This postcard from around 1911 reveals the splendour of the interior of the Runnacleave Private Hotel and Boarding House, which was opened in July 1891. Passing through the imposing iron and glass entrance hall, complete with palms, hanging lamps and carpet, the lounge hall was reached through double doors of 'Cathedral tinted lead lights'.

The reading room, separate ladies' drawing room and large billiard room were some of the many facilities provided at the Runnacleave. On Whit Monday 1892, the magnificent Runnacleave Hall was opened adjacent to the hotel, capable of seating 500 persons. It was a popular venue for concerts, 'private theatricals' and dances. D'Oyley Carte's Opera Company performed here on 12 July 1893.

The Granville Hotel, opened in June 1891, was named after one of the leading figures of the temperance movement. This picture was probably taken soon after it was completed as there seems to be work still going on in the new road. Southern Slopes were then allotments for the Ilfracombe Hotel.

This is Mrs Gardner's Boarding House at the top of Somers Crescent, before it became the Montebello Hotel. In 1892, having acquired and pulled down the adjoining cottages, £5,000 was spent on a magnificent six storey building with good views and hot and cold water on every landing.

The Crescent Hotel in Fore Street, now The Altro, was started as a small concern in 1883 by Mrs Lewis, a widow with young children. It expanded a few years later when Sir James Meek's house and gardens were sold and was known for its 'extreme civility and cleanliness'. The large porch feature can still be seen from Wilder Road.

The Belgrave Hotel, now the Berkeley Hotel, was built around 1884. It was the largest building designed by architect Mr Robins in 'warm tint buff bricks'. Seen here in the 1890s 'its luxurious appliances were skilfully managed' by Mr Richard Cross.

'Good diggings' is written on this postcard sent on 28 July 1909. As more and more people from all classes of society had the opportunity for a holiday, it seemed that any residents in the town who had a spare room to let made it available to supplement their income.

This may have been Ilfracombe's first holiday camp, pictured here in 1911. Situated in an enviable position high above the town, possibly in meadows near the present college, newly-arrived visitors had to report to the 'office' in the tent on the left. Other camps took place on Hillsborough and there was some concern that rates ought to be paid.

The original building on the site of the Royal Clarence Hotel in the High Street was the home of Dr Isaac Clarke, who in 1801 kept a pack of hounds. When he sold, it became Sutton's hotel, which kept the name for sixty-five years. Other owners included Edwin Reaves and then Richard Lake who ran a coach business from there.

Later advertised as a 'Family and Commercial Hotel', the Royal Clarence offered a drawing room for the ladies, a first class billiards room and this public lounge bar.

Four

Enjoy the Ride

The Duchess of Clarence, later Queen Adelaide, was the most notable person to enjoy the ride to Ilfracombe. In 1828 she changed carriages at Reaves Hotel, which prompted Mr Reave to rename it the Royal Clarence. This scene is dated 1876 as Thomas the Jewellers, situated next to the hotel, was built that year and the scaffolding is still visible.

The official opening of the Barnstaple and Ilfracombe Railway on 21 July 1874 was celebrated with triumphal floral arches all around the town. This one was erected in the High Street looking towards Portland Street. It was a day of great celebration with thousands of people pouring into town by road, rail and sea.

The erection of a shelter at the station in 1892 was necessary due to its elevated position above the town, where westerly gales caused considerable discomfort to passengers on the exposed platforms.

Visitors arriving at the station could have their luggage taken to their accommodation by carters, shown here in 1922. Passengers had a choice of horse-drawn cabs and omnibuses at this time, which were available for every train. Special by-laws were in force with strict rules of conduct and prices.

The *West Country* class 34032 can be seen leaving Ilfracombe on its way up to Mortehoe, the gradient being 1 in 36. Direct through services were provided from Waterloo and Paddington taking about five and a quarter hours in 1915. By the 1950s, 10,000 holidaymakers used the line each Saturday in the height of the season. However, passenger traffic declined and complete closure came in 1970.

Sam Colwill, Coach Proprietor, 96 High Street, is seen here with his famous Lynton coach *Benita* with her four white horses. He drove the first coach to Lynton in 1854 for Messrs Pridham and Lake and during the winters he handled the mail coaches to Barnstaple.

Copp's coach company was in competition on the opposite side of the road to Colwills, next to the Royal Clarence. Thomas Copp had first come to work for his uncle, Richard Lake, as foreman in charge of the posting hotel's horses and men. The driver was Tom Hussell and the guard Jan Robins.

'All aboard for trips to Barnstaple and Woolacombe'. A photographer was often outside the Bath House to take a picture before the coach left so that on its return, passengers could purchase them. Onlookers always liked to join in.

Ready for the journey back home, Sam Colwill's son Tom is the driver here and Bert Gear the guard. Bert, Les Gear's father, was famous for winning the horn-blowing contest at the Lynton Pony Show and Industrial Fair in 1906.

Private carriages could be hired for use about the town, such as this pony and trap seen outside the Victoria Pavilion in around 1900. The young lad in his work clothes and dilapidated boots holding the pony's reins is in complete contrast to the girl's smart outfit.

This delightful family with the two young girls in their elaborate hats, probably their 'Sunday best', enjoy their donkey ride on Capstone Parade in the early 1900s. Donkeys could be hired from many parts of the town, including the stand in the High Street under the high bank opposite where Pedlars shop is now.

A collection of pony traps and donkey chairs are pictured outside the Runnacleave Hotel on 9 September 1896, along with other visitors, many on donkeys. Donkey chairs, often used for the infirm, were like 'big arm chairs' with a hood for protection from sun or rain. Hotel staff can be seen peeping out of the windows.

Horse-drawn carriages complete with driver were available for hire to take visitors on trips to Lee and other local places of interest. This particular vehicle was available daily at 10.15 a.m. and 2.45 p.m. and can be seen with its passengers on 31 August 1899 outside Bath Cottage, which was available for rent as indicated on the poster.

The last coach-and-four ran in 1910, before the motor vehicle took over with day trips to more distant destinations. Excessive speeds of twelve miles per hour were reported. Colwill's smart charabancs, with their solid tyres and hoods if it rained, still left from the High Street Office.

Copp's booking office for Silver Cars had moved across the road between the Baptist Church and Oliver's shoe shop by the time this postcard was sent in 1919. The pneumatic tyres gave for a more comfortable ride.

Gathered on the pier in 1922 is Colwill's entire fleet of Grey Cars. A suitable one could be found for almost any occasion and they could be hired daily, making the whole of North Devon more accessible to visitors.

Taking a ride on the local bus going up Oxford Grove can only be imagined with horror today. The sender of this 1914 postcard was full of praise for the drivers. The tree-lined grove of smart town houses was built in 1872.

Mr W.H. Gubb's fleet of six-cylinder Violet Cars are lined up outside the Methodist Church in Wilder Road ready for an outing. Every opportunity was taken to advertise the charabanc company, whose headquarters were at The Lucky Horse Shoe, 133 High Street. During the First World War the government commandeered their coaches.

Ilfracombe Motors Ltd, as advertised, were the first company to take trips to Clovelly. The ladies on this omnibus are well wrapped up with rugs and muffs for what must have been a very cold journey in winter or early spring.

Five

What Shall We Do Today?

The beaches were a big attraction for holidaymakers and catching the ferry from the quay was an easy way to reach Rapparee beach. There was also access by a footpath and when the landowner tried to charge £10 annual rent in 1860, Sir Bourchier Wrey insisted it should be a public right of way with free bathing.

Alf Price had a flourishing business hiring out deckchairs and bathing huts. In 1878 he had a set-to with Prince Frederick William of Prussia, grandson of Queen Victoria, who was throwing stones at his father's bathing huts. They went at it 'hammer and tongs' and ever after boasted that he had given the future Kaiser a 'bloody nose'.

The latest arrivals on the Rapparee Ferry in 1911 are very interested in the antics of youngsters using the boat launcher as a diving board. Mixed bathing was only allowed 'under suitable conditions' from 1906. Prior to this, a flag was hoisted on the slopes of Hillsborough to show when the beach was reserved for ladies use only.

There was always something of interest to see when strolling around the harbour. The craft with the prominent sail was the pleasure yacht the *Monarch*, which set sail in August 1887 with twenty-two on board. When level with the Tunnels, she was caught in an unexpected storm, swamped and sank with heavy loss of life.

These steep steps, fondly known as Jacob's Ladder, stretched from the Cove up towards Larkstone Terrace. Beatrix Potter may have used this route down to the harbour when she and her family stayed at Hillsborough Terrace in 1882. The ladder was removed in 1969 when the Cove Road and car park were built.

Mr Alex Campbell, accompanied by a group of ladies and children, can be seen on board a sailing vessel in the outer harbour. In the 1880s he ran the Campbell Pier Hotel, seen to the right of the boat. In 1893 the hotel and the Golden Lion next door, a favourite hostelry for boatmen, were demolished and the new Pier Hotel was built.

It has been suggested that Mr Frank Tuck, holding the gun on board the *Ripple* in around 1900, may have had the task of using it to start a yacht race. He certainly seems to be dressed for an occasion and regattas were held regularly. Nichol Barbeary was the boatman standing in the stern.

In holiday mood, these 1950s holidaymakers were able to enjoy one of many trips and motor cruises available along the spectacular coast eastward to Combe Martin and westward to Lee Bay. There was also a good choice of rowing and sailing boats for hire by the hour or day.

This family arrived back safely from their outing with an experienced boatman, unlike the story in the 1906 *Chronicle* of a Mr Pickett and some of his children who were 'upset' from a boat near the pier. Mr Pickett dived in to rescue one of the younger children. Fortunately they were none the worse for their ordeal.

The pier has always been a place to gather for events as this photograph taken soon after its opening in 1873 shows. The phrenologist would tell your fortune by feeling the bumps on your head and the armchair weighing machine was the latest model.

This was the view from around 1870 when walking down from Lantern Hill, with Cheyne Beach below and Capstone to the right. The church is St Philip and St James' and Coronation Terrace, with the Assembly Rooms in the middle, is above the open-grassed area top left.

Cheyne beach was popular with Victorian marine life collectors who liked to gather specimens of anemones, due to the influence of naturalist Philip Henry Gosse. To improve access to Cheyne beach, it was proposed in 1905 to make a cutting through the rock with a bridge over it at an estimated cost of £150.

This path leads from Capstone Crescent to Ropery Meadow on the seafront, where in this view of 1910 the Gaiety Theatre is just being built at the end of the Promenade Terrace. The spire of the Methodist church can be seen in the distance with the Torrs behind.

The Local Board purchased the area called Ropery Meadow, shown in front of the Victoria Pavilion, for £2,203 in 1872. Mr Edward Joseph had so enjoyed his stay in Ilfracombe that he presented an ornamental drinking fountain in 1890. It was removed in 1922 when the pleasure grounds were re-designed. The Ilfracombe Hotel can be seen in the background.

The Winter Pavilion, built in 1887 to commemorate the Golden Jubilee of Queen Victoria, was a great asset to the town. On wet or wintry days, visitors could shelter amongst the shrubs and climbing plants and be entertained by the bands or concert parties. A charge was only made for the best seats.

Victorian visitors loved to promenade along the sea front by Wildersmouth beach. Ilfracombe acquired a new bandstand next to the Pavilion at the cost of £350 in 1894. It was sold in 1970 for £150 and has recently been restored in the Midlands by a private owner. Professor Smith with his Punch and Judy show, pictured on the beach, was also very popular.

Holidaymakers on 10 June 1924 enjoyed listening to the 'season' band playing in the bandstand. A man would come round with a collecting box and probably more than one visitor pretended to be asleep!

Hundreds of people would join in the Sunday church parade, promenading around Capstone in their Sunday finery as shown here in around 1900. The parade was built by the unemployed during the difficult winter of 1842/43 for the wage of a loaf of bread and a shilling a day. Its opening was regarded as the 'dawning of prosperity' for the town.

People at the back of Capstone in the 1880s seem very intent on watching an event out to sea, sheltering from the sun under their umbrellas. It may have been a Lifeboat Day display similar to one reported in September 1893, when thousands lined Capstone Parade to watch a demonstration of rocket apparatus used for saving lives.

Ilfracombe Museum was opened in 1932 in the disused laundry of the Ilfracombe Hotel, which by then belonged to the Urban District Council. The first curator, Mervyn Grove Palmer, had travelled in South America as a young man collecting natural history specimens for the British Museum. The petrol pumps for the hotel vehicles can still be seen here in 1936.

Ilfracombe Zoo Park was opened in 1949 at Comyn Hill House, Worth Road. The owner Charles Trevisick is seen here holding a chimpanzee. The zoo boasted over five hundred animals and multi-coloured birds, several of them appearing on television with Wilfred Pickles.

The Ilfracombe Sea Bathing Company built the Bath House in 1836. Thomas Stabb, a surgeon who had recently moved to the town formed this company. It was built in a Greek revival style and provided hot and cold baths. The tunnel to the beach was also cut about this time. The hotel to the left is the Beacon Castle, which burned down in 1985.

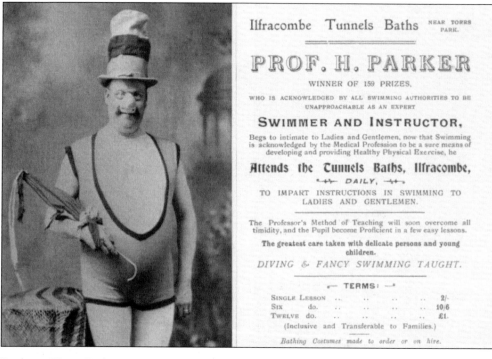

Professor Harry Parker, swimming instructor at the Tunnels, is seen here dressed ready for a carnival. He had won many prizes in competition swimming in the Thames. He was known as 'England's greatest natatorial artist' when he gave daring displays at the pier and Ilfracombe Hotel swimming baths.

The Tunnels Beaches were approached through a series of tunnels carved out of the rock by Welsh miners in around 1836. This lithograph of the ladies' bathing beach was published in around 1850, and until 1906 there were separate pools for ladies and gentlemen. A bugler was appointed as a lookout to watch for anyone who strayed into the wrong area.

The view from above the Bath House on the way to Torrs Walk is before 1884, as neither the Belgrave Hotel nor Belgrave Terrace, later the Osborne Hotel, have been built. Sandringham Villas are the only houses on this part of Wilder Road.

Looking back, while climbing higher up to the Torrs, reveals a panoramic view taken before 1888. Torre House, now Merlin Court, is the building on the left. Notice the absence of the Victoria Pavilion and Runnacleave Hotel.

After paying a toll of one penny in 1888, visitors could take the Torrs Walk over the succession of hills known as 'the Alps of England'. The path zigzagged up the hillside to the highest Torr giving magnificent views of the coast and sea.

At the summit, shown here in 1894, the Torrs Pavilion and restaurant provided a welcome sight for ramblers and 'good Devonshire fare' was available. It even provided a carriage home for those too weary to continue. The Pavilion was demolished in 1964.

Leaving the Pavilion, walkers could either retrace their steps to the entrance, return to town via Torrs Park or continue along the main path to Lee, over hills covered with ferns and wild flowers. Lee was known as the 'valley of fuchsias'.

This undated event took place in the grounds of Langleigh House. Admiral Down, a contemporary of Nelson, once owned this beautiful secluded estate. He planted trees here to commemorate the celebrated naval battle off Cape St Vincent. The trees were arranged in the order in which the British fleet went into action.

Hillsborough, 447ft high, shown in this print published in around 1837 by J. Banfield Library of Ilfracombe, has always been a favourite place for visitors to gain the best views of the harbour. Storm shelters were built on Hillsborough to serve as a refuge from sudden squalls.

The Hillsborough estate, extending from Rapparee Cove to Hele Bay, was purchased for £7,500 in June 1895 by the Ilfracombe District Council. In May 1920 the council agreed to allow a Mr W.H. Widden to erect a refreshment room, which was a welcome stop on a walk to Hele.

In 1897 the stream that flows onto Hele beach actually ran openly down the middle of the approach road. Hele, at the turn of the century, was a pretty little hamlet with about thirty cottages, a village school, Hele Hotel and Lewis' tearooms.

The ketch *Emily* was built in Jersey and owned by Captain Jack Irwin. She is seen here unloading coal on the beach at Hele for domestic use and also for the gas works that opened in 1904.

A mill at Hele existed as early as 1525 and still survives today. The millponds were reported to be full of eels and were caught in a wicker trap set above the water wheel. During the Second World War the millstones were used to grind up animal feed. These children are seen here at Little Town Farm, Hele.

Six

A Stroll Through the Town

A stroll through the town begins in the High Street at the junction with Northfield Road. It was a busy thoroughfare in 1904 and advertisements described the handsome houses, some elegantly furnished as lodgings, and fashionable shops with attendants who treated purchasers with the utmost civility.

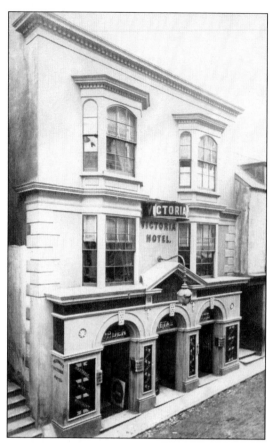

The original Victoria Hotel was built on this site in 1834, the bay windows and frontage being added in the late nineteenth century. An 1883 trade directory gives Arthur Huxtable, a wine and spirit merchant, as the owner. In those days, the owners had their names embossed on the beer bottles.

William Furse started business as a basket maker in Market Street. He later moved to these premises, part of Ilfracombe Town Hall, built in 1862. He purchased the building from the council in 1931 for £4,000 when they moved to new offices in the Ilfracombe Hotel.

Samuel and William Day owned the land at the bottom of Oxford Grove where the old fish market had been. In 1873 they built new shops and offices and entered into an agreement with the Local Board for a clock tower to be incorporated into their plans. The Great Western Hotel was demolished and rebuilt as the New Christ Church in 1939. It was converted into the Embassy cinema in 1948 and is now the Pendle Stairway to the Stars Cinema.

71

Ludgate House was built in 1890 for the sole purpose of being the grand department store of J. Pugsley & Son. It could supply every item necessary to furnish an entire home, and included accommodation for their shop assistants on the top floor. This building in the High Street is now occupied by Spar.

J. Pugsley & Son issued this beautifully illustrated invoice, dated 7 July 1904, to Mrs Pope of Oxford Park for the renovation of a bonnet at a cost of two shillings.

Clarks Chemist and Dentist, No. 23 High Street, was by 1893 owned by Mr Thornley. Because of rebuilding and renumbering in the High Street it is sometimes difficult to identify properties today. Clarks became Locketts Chemist, and the Moon Inn on the right was demolished in around 1890 and Worcester House, now Pedlar's, was built.

A late nineteenth-century trade directory shows that Frank Carthew owned the Queens, a family and commercial hotel and posting establishment. He was also in the coaching business with Thomas Copp. The building itself had been on this site at the top of Northfield Road since the mid-1700s.

Mr Myatt is standing in the doorway of his wonderful store, which he stocked with every desirable stationery item a Victorian would require. His shop opposite the Queens Hotel became Vinces Library, which was demolished in the 1930s to make way for the new gas showroom, now the council offices.

In the 1900s Colwill's Railway Hotel was right next door to the surviving Wellington Arms. The left-hand-side of the building eventually became part of Somerfield and the entrance to the stabling area can still be seen between this supermarket and the estate agents.

Here is Church Street as it looked at the time of the railway's arrival, with a variety of cottages, the Ring 'O Bells public house just around the corner, cobbled paths and a narrow dirt road. The building on the right was replaced by Skinner & Squires in 1905 and eventually became the main part of Somerfield.

An unusual photograph of the late 1870s showing men still demolishing cottages. The wall of Winsham Terrace can be seen on the left but the whole lower end of Church Street has been swept away. The Alpha Hotel was built on the corner of Wilder Road and the terrace known as Northcote Buildings was completed in 1880.

Eli Hill, a coachbuilder, had premises at 21-22 Church Street, on the corner of Horne Road. In the *Ilfracombe Chronicle*, 3 September 1887, he advertised 'Ilfracombe coach factory promises best workmanship and well-seasoned materials guaranteed'. Eli retired in 1908 and died eight years later.

This interesting scene of various trade carts and horses was taken after 1880 when the Marland brick premises on the right were built. The walled garden of the church had not been dreamed of as a War Memorial and the little boy collecting the horse manure little knew what the motorcar would do to his trade.

Holy Trinity Parish Church with the War Memorial Gardens were photographed soon after they had been created in 1922. Trinity Rooms on the right was built in 1862 and used as a schoolroom and a working men's club. It replaced the original Church House that had been used as the Poor House since the mid-1600s.

Part of the graveyard at the Parish Church shows the memorial of John Toms who organized the building of Capstone Parade in 1843. His fellow townsmen erected the obelisk in his memory, deliberately on a spot in the churchyard where at the time Capstone was visible.

John Mill Chanter, vicar of Holy Trinity Church, Ilfracombe, from 1836 for over fifty years, was married to Charles Kingsley's sister Charlotte. The church was described by his daughter Gratiana in her *Wanderings in North Devon* as being in a 'terrible tumble-down condition; filled with high worm-eaten pews, horse boxes and five galleries, crowding and darkening the church in a most unsightly manner'.

This elegant lych-gate at the top of Church Hill was dedicated in 1894 to the memory of John Mill Chanter. The old lych-gate had been at the top of the steps by the poor house and to the left of them was situated the town stocks which, tradition says, mazed John Lucimore threw into the sea.

The view from Cairn Road shows Ilfracombe expanding up St Brannocks Road with one house still under construction. There is a fair on the open land just before the point where the road divides. The railway station can just be seen behind the tree on the left.

Richard Bligh, described as a landed proprietor of houses, and his wife Ann, provided Score Church and burial ground in 1855. It was a token of their love for their Christian brethren of all denominations.

The original road leading to the Torrs Walk was by a lane near the east entrance of the churchyard. Mr Camp was the proprietor of the land and at one time there was a tollhouse in Osborne Road.

These beautiful newly-built villas from around 1896, and with their original names, are from left to right: Regency, Torrs Vale and Glen Tor, Southcliffe, Wessex, Hereford House and Parkroyd. The hills behind were later planted with trees to complete this Victorian suburb that was designed by architects Gould, Robins, Oliver and Hussell over a period of fifty years.

The Ilfracombe Joint Stock Land and Investment Company was formed by a group of local businessmen in 1860. Their aim was to develop the land on the southern slopes of the Torrs, which was sunny, protected from north-west winds and had good views over the Wilder Valley. These handsome Marland brick-built dwellings are on the Upper Torrs.

Taking a closer look at Roslyn Hoe, now called St Martins, shows that Robins' symmetrical design of the 1880s was particularly elegant. Many high-ranking personnel chose to live in the desirable Torrs Park development. An 1890 newspaper, which listed the occupants, included a major, a colonel, a captain and an admiral.

The Ilfracombe Methodist church, built for £5,000, was opened on the 12 July 1898. This is now the Emmanuel Church. The site at the bottom of Market Street previously housed the lower portion of the old market that had been demolished. The Wesleyan Methodists had exchanged, with the council, their old site in Ropery Meadow for this one. The Hotel Alexandra got its name when part of the market building became the Alexandra Theatre.

This view looking towards the town from Capstone is before 1892 as there is no Montebello Hotel visible at the top of Somers Crescent, but it is after 1885 as the Arcade is already built. The terrace at the top of the picture is Montpelier and the row of Promenade boarding houses were constructed around 1890.

Seen from Capstone this view, with the second Wesleyan Chapel constructed in 1863, was taken around 1892. Rupertswood Terrace in the centre, situated below Coronation Terrace, was still being built. Lee Place beyond the Chapel was the site of the rope-spinning sheds of this nineteenth-century industry. Ropery Meadow gained its name because the rope-making path could be extended through this open area as far as Bath House.

Capstone House was built into the hillside in 1837, opposite St Philip and St James' Church. It was a fairly plain Georgian design with the garden at the front. The bay windows with the fancy ironwork would have been added in late Victorian times when it became a boarding house.

Look! No cars! The names are still familiar, the Royal Britannia and the Crown Inn, now The Sandpiper, but they have undergone many alterations since this 1890s picture was taken. Pophams Boarding Establishment can just be seen on the left with their grocers shop beneath.

A vanished view at the end of Broad Street before turning right into Fore Street with Rupertswood Terrace just visible above. In the centre is Webbers haircutting and shaving room complete with barber's pole, and on the left is Kelly's Old Curiosity Shop.

Cobbled courtyards and dilapidated cottages off Broad Street were a stark contrast to the elegant hotels and shops of the late nineteenth century. The Housing for the Working Classes Act of 1890 urged councils to clear away unsanitary dwellings that were unfit for human habitation and to build council estates. It took until 1933 for this to begin in Ilfracombe.

Morris' rag-and-bone shop was on the right at the bottom of Fore Street. Next door, Mrs Ann Morris ran the Marine Store and earthenware dealer shop. From a passing circus, the family once bought a horse called Beauty, which the Town Crier later owned.

The Ebrington Arms was one of eight public houses or beer shops in Fore Street in the 1800s. Some still exist today, others are names not even remembered, New Inn, Hope & Anchor, Concord Inn, William the Fourth, Ship & Castle also known as The Gander, Prince of Wales and the George & Dragon.

The Comer family complete with Grandma have stepped outside their butchers shop in Fore Street to pose for the photographer. Many members of this family earned their living from the sea, and the tombstone records give accounts of at least three sad cases of drowning in the family.

Photographs of Mr W. Cole's premises on the corner of Fore Street and Portland Street, before and after the great fire of 1896, have often been published. Here, however, is a picture of his original shop taken before 1888 when his new five-storey multi-purpose business was built.

The Free Church named Christ Church was built in 1844 and Reverend Benjamin Price looked after the ministry for fifty years. The sad remains of the 1891 improved design are here ready for demolition to widen Portland Street. Plans had been proposed for this in 1931 and the Church moved to the High Street, but widening was not carried out until the 1960s.

Castle House, built in the eighteenth century, commands a grand view over the harbour. Some mystery still surrounds the exact position of a fort or castle mentioned in the Civil War encounters. A map published in 1876 by W. Stewert clearly shows a castle in the area of lower Worth Road, but eighteenth-century painters have included one in the vicinity of Castle House.

Nos 1 and 2 Larkstone Terrace were up for auction on Wednesday 5 June 1872, described as 'recently erected freehold properties with splendid views, three sitting rooms, ten bedrooms, three water closets and a yearly fee farm rent of £4 12s'. These and the rest of the terrace were built with their backs to the road to take full advantage of their position overlooking the harbour.

The Price family, whose son was famous for his tussle with the Kaiser, once owned the thatched cottage at the bottom of Chambercombe Road. Now it is a public house called the Thatched Inn. One of its memorable owners was an American named Charles Disney.

In the 1870s the villas in Hostle Park were the homes of master mariners, men of the cloth and gentlemen of independent means. This fine example 'Paou Shun', incidentally the name of a merchant sailing ship of that period, is now part of the Edenmore nursing home complex.

An 1888 map clearly shows that the Marlborough Club, opposite Somerfields in the High Street, was once known as Winsham House, and adjoining it going up the hill was Highfield House which now forms part of the snooker area of the club.

Seven

Meet the Locals

Visitors to the town have always been assured of a warm welcome. Leslie Passmore, advertising himself as 'The Tie King', was always pleased to see his customers at No. 24 High Street. He sold 'dainty and novel presents' at reasonable prices. This promotional card is dated before 1911 when the High Street was re-numbered.

Mr Benjamin Luxmoore, remembered in the town as the owner of a drapers and furnishers shop, is seen here with his family at their home in Hostle Park. From left to right, back row: J.M. Luxmoore, B.M. Luxmoore, Winifred. Front row: Gladys, Benjamin Luxmoore, Hester, May.

Luxmoore & Sons, now Drapers, opened in 1888 and rapidly expanded. The 6½d bazaar was added on next door in 1931. Mr Luxmoore was still working at the age of eighty-four years when his shop celebrated its Golden Jubilee in August 1938. Note the sign of the Masonic Hall above, which was in use from 1888.

Mr Walter George Coats of 'Coat's Dairy' moved to No. 12 Northfield Road between 1910 and 1914, having had a business in the High Street for many years. He advertised milk, home cooking and cream on his milk churns. Locals will remember the existence of Coat's Dairy until the 1980s.

'Join the Stores and share our Profit', so says the familiar Co-operative Society slogan seen here in 1919 at No. 83 High Street, now Jeffreys Newsagent. Standing in the entrance is the manager Mr Prout with his staff, including the lad with the hand-delivery basket on wheels.

George Edward Russell ran a China tea mart and Colonial produce warehouse in Portland Street in the 1870s. In around 1879 he transferred his grocery business to No. 14 High Street, next to the Market Arches, where it extended right through to Market Square. His Chinese assistant would have been something of a novelty in those days.

There were many butcher shops all with their own slaughterhouses nearby. J.H. Smith & Son, pictured here in around 1922, was at No. 137 High Street, now unrecognisable as Barclays Bank on the corner of Oxford Grove. In the doorway are, from left to right: Mrs J.H. Smith, Miss Flossie Smith, Eileen (later Mrs E. Pedlar), Jean Smith.

Oxford Park and Nursery shown in the 1890s, was situated near the top of Oxford Grove and owned by Mr J. Braund at that time. It was open at a nominal fee for the public's pleasure. The park was laid out with a fountain, fishpond, statues of Flora and Venus and three tennis courts. Beside eight greenhouses, there were twenty-one beehives.

Under the watchful eye of the head gardener, Mr Pike, chrysanthemums were a speciality grown in one of the glasshouses at Oxford Grove. Note there are vines above. A vast variety of flowers including orchids, as well as tomatoes, cucumbers and even peaches were cultivated and sent to Mr Herbert Braund's shop in the High Street.

The Rosebud maypole dancers of the Juvenile Rechabite Society entertained in the Runnacleave Hall on 15 March 1898. Sister Lily Wilson, centre, was the Queen. Misses Pugsley played a pianoforte duet, a medley of nursery rhymes was sung and the band performed. The Rechabites were founded as a Friendly Society to provide some security before the days of state benefits.

Joan Collins, second row up, third from the right, attended Hereford House School in Torrs Park as a daygirl in 1941, when she, her mother and younger sister Jackie were evacuated to Ilfracombe. The two Principals were Miss Doris Theak, with Bogey the cat, and Miss Ethel Theak holding Brindle the dog.

Mr Fred Lord was head of St Philip and St James' School from 1887 until 1929. He was progressive for his time and organized instructive visits to businesses including the Gas Works, Steam Laundry and the Electric Light and Power Company where on 8 March 1912 his pupils were given mild shocks from a four-volt accumulator!

These youngsters were learning to swim under Mr Lord's watchful eye in the Bath House pool in 1916. His new training methods were published in *Teachers World* on 13 April 1921. They included a long cord tied to a band round the waist to 'haul' a child across the bath and using bicycle and motor inner tubes as buoyancy aids.

There must have been great excitement on the evening of Wednesday 10 September 1927 when the winners of the FA Challenge Cup and the Welsh Cup, Cardiff City, came to Ilfracombe to play a friendly with the local team. Their two 'beautiful' trophies were on display. Mr Tom Edwards, the gentleman wearing the bowler hat, was a reporter with the *Ilfracombe Chronicle*.

Ilfracombe Secondary School rugby team 1931/32. From left to right, back row: Rowswell, Gray, Rendell, Delve, Sweetman, Kelly, Lewis. Middle row: Wood, Sanders, Fainlight, Challacombe, Morcom, Gough, Cooke. Front row: Tonkinson, Page.

The band of the 1st Devonshire Volunteer Artillery Corps in the 1890s. From left to right, back row: Charles Rose, W. Beer, ? Rumson, Fred Delve, A.G. Snow, W. Allen, Fred Challacombe. Middle row: G. Burnell, W. Sanders, Frank Offer, J. Challen (bandmaster), Ernest Price, G. Pile, Nat Vellacott, Walter Jones. Front row: Joe Backaller, W.J. Webber, Frank Becker, Geo Harris, C. Rose.

This local Edwardian wedding party from around 1910 is believed to have a connection with the Gear family. The bridesmaid on the left was Elsie Millman and the one on the right Florrie Drake. Batten of Capstone Studio photographed them in someone's backyard with a tartan rug as a backcloth and a carpet laid underfoot.

John Bushen was ninety years old when this photograph was taken in October 1943. He was the oldest first class licensed boatman in Ilfracombe, and very proud that he had been a lifeboat volunteer for forty years. He had been up and down the Bristol Channel 'hundreds of times' during his sea-faring life.

Harbour staff down on the pier in 1946. From left to right, back row: Bill Williams, Bill Fisher, Fred Rudd, Reg Nunn, Tom Pears, Fred Comer, Albert Hussell. Front row: Captain George Burfitt (harbour master), F.G. Reed (harbour committee chairman), Jan Wilson (harbour constable).

Bill Lewis, a Hele fisherman, accompanied by his granddaughter May and grandson Billy, was very proud to pose with these kegs of coconut oil, which he had recovered from the sea at Hele Bay in around 1918. As salvage, these kegs brought a reward of £10, a great deal of money in those days.

The Ilfracombe postal staff, seen here around 1900, will have included Mr S.T. Balment who started as a messenger boy in 1887, progressed to a postal clerk, telegraphist and then manager until he retired forty-six years later. Apparently there was a resident parrot, and the introduction of girls in 1898 to serve behind the counter was considered shocking.

The Ilfracombe Boys Life Brigade Unit was formed in November 1923 with twelve members and by February 1924 had forty. It was attached to the Wesleyan Church. Drill played an important role and was a means of maintaining discipline. These mischievous-looking members completed a first aid course in June 1925.

The elephants are 'meeting the locals' in June 1931 outside F.C. Snell, Wine and Spirit Merchants at 3 High Street, later to become the Prince Albert public house. They were annual visitors from the circus and the keg of beer was a welcome treat. Can you imagine this happening today?

Eight

What Shall We Do Tonight?

Visitors could see concerts, the music hall, plays and variety shows in the new concert hall, which replaced the central glass section of the Victoria Pavilion. Constructed at a cost of £8,000, it opened on 18 May 1925. Many stars performed there including Alma Cogan and Bill Maynard, who topped the bill in 1954. The 'Farewell Performance' took place in September 1997.

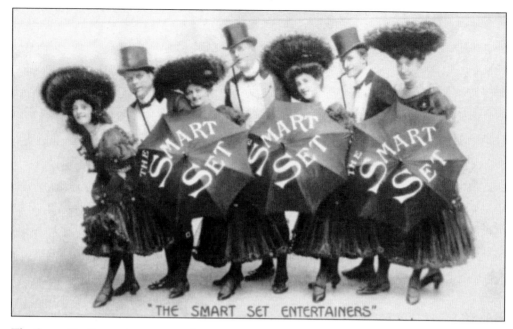

The Smart Set Entertainers were a favourite concert party 'appearing once again' in the Pavilion during the summer of 1908. Their many talents included singing, dancing and impersonations, and they provided a 'constantly moving picture of colour and graceful gyration'.

Many people in the town will remember the dances that took place in the Victoria Pavilion during the Second World War with the British and American troops who were billeted locally.

The Alexandra Theatre was considered a fine concert and dance hall, and could seat 1,400. It was situated in the lower part of the Alexandra Hall behind what is now Emmanuel Church. Constructed in 1901, it was named after Queen Alexandra, wife of King Edward VII. During the Second World War it was known as the Garrison Theatre.

Ilfracombe Choral Society performed the *Messiah* in the opening year of the Alexandra Theatre. Other shows included plays by the Ilfracombe Players and the Pioneer Pay Corp during the 1940s, *Murder Mistaken* direct from the Vaudeville Theatre, London, in August 1953 and the Operatic Society musical *Gipsy Brown* with Esme Preston in 1957.

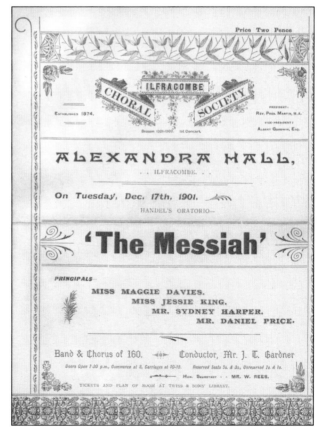

There was, and still is, an amazing amount of local talent in Ilfracombe. These youngsters, known as 'The Cavallo Royal Marine Theatrical Group' are dressed to perform *Nell*. They were connected with Luigi Cavallo, the proprietor of The Royal Marine Sanitary Steam Laundry, who also advertised his 'carpet beating machine' in 1904.

The Trial of Kit Boniface took place at the Runnacleave Hall on 6 May 1897. A serious charge of enticing people into saloons for the purpose of drinking was levied against the prisoner. Characters included the Lord Chief Justice Fairman, Counsel for the prosecution Messrs Searcham and Ferrett and witness Robert Ruffanreddy, a pedlar.

The Picture Hall in Northfield Road was opened in 1911 in the upper floor of the Rechabites meeting place. There were 150 tip-up armchairs, electric lights throughout and unlike many entertainments it was to be open all year round. The building is decked out to celebrate the Coronation of King George V, with Laurel and Hardy topping the bill.

Apart from the latest film the cinema also had resident entertainers in the form of a duet of singers and dancers called the 'Two Mervyns'. The usherette on the right is Annie Morris whose parents owned the rag-and-bone shop in Fore Street. In the 1920s it was renamed the Empire Cinema and finally The New Cinema which closed in 1951.

The Ilfracombe Hotel swimming baths, situated at the end of the hotel promenade, was a great attraction for guests when it opened in 1880. It held 178,000 gallons of seawater, changed daily by use of a steam pump. There were sixty dressing rooms and an experienced swimming master and mistress were in 'constant attendance'.

Galas and 'aquatic entertainment' organized by the Ilfracombe Swimming Club were very popular at the baths. This 1892 event featured races for men and boys, a display of ornamental swimming, diving by the swimming mistress Miss Belle White, cork bobbing in top hats and comic tub races. Even the town band played!

Ginnett's Hippodrome and Circus came to town in April 1893. It was considered to be one of the oldest and best 'equestrian establishments' with 200 horses, and artists including ten clowns and performing elephants. The schoolchildren would have a half-day holiday and the opening parade processed through the High Street before the performances in St Brannocks Road at 2.30 p.m. and 7.45 p.m. Prices of admission ranged from the posh seats in the carpeted stalls for 3 shilings, and the 'area' 6d. At the afternoon performance all schoolchildren were admitted for 2d each.

The Imperial Hotel Pierrot team: Misses Bostock, Washington Smith, M. and W. Thompson and Mr Shellabear, seen here outside the hotel, won the best tableaux in a novel 'bicycle gymkhana' held on 15 August 1901 at Langleigh House in aid of the town band. There was a fun programme of bicycle sports, followed by a parade through the town to the Alexandra Theatre.

Having completed a contract to lay pipes under the pier, the diving firm was asked to participate in the Carnival on 29 August 1904. Their 'King Neptune' float gained joint fourth prize. From left to right, back row: J. Blackmore, W. Ward, F. Wallis (Neptune), J. Wells, J. White. Middle row: W. Burgess (Diver), C. White (Chief Diver). Front row: W. Wilcox, G. Ley.

Eric Hutchings, a local auctioneer on the right, and Bruce Reed, undertaker, seen at Brimlands, won first prize at the Carnival with their 'Johnnie Walker' entry. Note the whisky bottles on the running board and the Johnnie Walker plaque. The procession was the highlight of the Regatta event, taking place on 12-13 August 1931.

The Ilfracombe Bathing Belles tableau entered the Carnival on 20 August 1953. From left to right, back row: Elizabeth Bennetto, -?- , Pamela Lewis (standing). Front row: Margaret Rumsam, -?-. A record amount of £275 was collected. Perhaps the 'NO WAITING THIS SIDE TODAY' sign was easier to enforce in the 1950s!

GENERAL TOM THUMB.

P.T. Barnum discovered Charles S. Stratton, famously known as General Tom Thumb. When this lithograph was produced in 1844 he was six years old and just twenty-five inches tall. In 1865, two years after his marriage to Lavinia Warren, and accompanied by their infant daughter, they visited Ilfracombe as part of a tour of England. They performed twice at the Town Hall on 16 December. Their miniature carriage can be seen in The National Trust collection at Arlington Court.

Nine

Times of Change

Ilfracombe High Street was formed along a steep sloping hillside with the original houses on the south side built up on banks. With the increase of coach and horse transport in the 1890s, it became necessary to remove the banks in order to widen the road. The demolition work is to the left of where Turton's butchers shop is now.

Compass Hill was described in 1893 as 'eighteen ancient dilapidated cottages piled on top of each other, some with no water closets and most with defective drainage'. Slops and refuse were emptied over the cliff where it remained until washed or blown away. Ilfracombe prided itself on health so there were concerns that a remedy should be found before typhoid or cholera struck. However it was pointed out by residents that the hill was not unhealthy as three of the oldest women in Devonshire lived there. The issue was still being discussed in 1904.

The provision of pure clean water became an important issue during the nineteenth century as Ilfracombe developed as a health resort. This view of the two reservoirs in the Slade Valley, with the railway line on the right, was taken in 1904. Utilising the water from the West Wilder Brook, the upper reservoir was built in 1866 and the second in 1887.

These local dignitaries, posing on a bridge at Slade in around 1904, were probably celebrating the arrival of pure water from the headwaters of the River Bray at Challacombe on Exmoor, by means of fourteen miles of pipeline. This was achieved after The Ilfracombe Improvement Act was passed in Parliament in 1900. Water rates were 1s 6d in the pound.

Quayfield House was situated on Hillsborough Road next to Castle House. In the 1851 census it was the home of Richard Bligh and his wife Anne who gave the land for St Philip and St James' Church. This view shows one of the triumphal arches erected for the opening of the railway in 1874 when Sir Bourchier Wrey was living there.

The Cliffe Hydro Hotel, which replaced Quayfield House, was opened on 1 July 1905 as a health spa inspired by the clean water Ilfracombe received. The baths were advertised as having installed 'electric radiant heat, high frequency and vibrating massage under medical supervision.' The motorbike and sidecar are captured here in around 1920.

W.H. Gubb & Sons are working on Hillsborough Terrace during the widening of Hillsborough Road in 1928. The improvements were necessary because of the increase in motorised vehicles, but had been a long time on the drawing board while discussions were made as to the financing by the Ministry of Transport and Devon County Council. The building in the centre was St Philip and St James' vicarage.

Looking towards Larkstone Terrace the road widening continued on to Watermouth Road and here at the junction of the road leading to the beach can be seen the narrowness and sweep of the original tree-lined route. Horse-drawn vehicles were still being used, including that of J.H. Hasking, Baker.

The Western Telephone gang, including Mr James Taylor seated centre, were working on laying underground 'telephonic lines' and the erection of poles in 1912. The Postmaster General asked for Council consent on 4 August 1911. The first telephone was installed with great success in 1888 at the office and yards of Lake & Copp, coach proprietors.

The Wilder Road tennis courts were converted into a 'pleasure ground', now known as Runnymede Gardens, in May 1949. Part of the Wilder Brook was diverted through the site under the guidance of the surveyor, Mr J. Westaway, and head gardener Mr F. Heard. It was felt that the completed gardens would enhance the view to the Southern Slopes.

Ten

Times to Remember

Special times to remember include this early photograph of the Victoria Pavilion, showing on the left Mr J.C. Clarke Senior, glazier of No. 87 High Street and his workmen, having just completed the installation of all the tinted window glass. After many delays, the 'shelter' or 'cucumber frame' as it was known, was opened to the public in August 1888.

Scenes of great celebration greeted Queen Victoria's Diamond Jubilee on Tuesday 22 June 1897. After a grand procession, the children, bands and friendly societies converged on Capstone Hill and Ropery Meadow with their banners. Conducted by Mr A. Wilshire, the children sang a patriotic song and waved their flags. Amidst loud cheering the Volunteer Artillery Corps then fired their guns.

The practice Battery for the Ilfracombe Volunteer Artillery Corps was situated on the eastern side of Hillsborough. The Corps was formed in 1859 and every member was required to attend an annual fifteen-day camp for battery training.

The Devonshire Regiment and their band, arriving in Ilfracombe on Friday 23 August 1895, marched past the Town Hall where the Chairman of the District Council, Mr T. Copp, waited on the temporary balcony to greet them. Everywhere was covered in bunting and spectators were packed thickly 'like sardines in a box'. Hopefully the man on the window ledge held on!

The camping ground at Hillsborough, placed at the disposal of the Devonshire Regiment, allowed them to recover from their route march from Plymouth, before embarking on the *Cambria* the next day bound for Newport. A local fund provided the men with a pint of beer, two ounces of Navy Cut tobacco and three quarters of a pound of plum pudding.

The Great Fire of Ilfracombe started at 12.40 a.m. on the night of 28 July 1896 in the basement of Mr William Cole's ironmongers and furniture shop on the corner of Portland Street and Fore Street. Due to a water shortage, the supply had been switched off overnight but despite this and a lack of pressure, the volunteer fire brigade managed to get it under control by the following morning.

The Arcade acted like a funnel and spread the fire right through it and the adjoining properties. Flames leapt across Portland Street and in total thirty-five houses and business premises and their contents were destroyed. Damage was estimated at between £80,000 and £100,000, most of which was borne by local insurance offices.

Messrs Twiss & Sons and Messrs Harding & Sons owned fourteen shops between them in the Arcade where they had sold photographic and printed souvenirs and fancy goods. The fire brigade's entire equipment was a manual Merryweather engine, a hose-reel cart and one telescopic ladder on wheels. Thankfully the weather that night was fine and calm.

Later that year, the 1896 fire brigade crew were presented with medals and £2 each at a dinner in their honour at the Royal Clarence Hotel. From left to right, back row: Walter Jewell, George Burnell, Thomas Knill, James Gumm, Thomas Williams, Richard Passmore. Middle row: John Nicholls, John Lewis, Captain Richard Jewell, Alfred Jeffrey, Alfred Gumm. Front row: Joseph Mock, William Duggleby, William Curtis. Not in the picture but presented were F. McKey and W. Nicholls.

Naval manoeuvres off Ilfracombe on Wednesday 13 July 1910 saw the second class cruiser *Bonaventure* carrying ten guns under the command of Frank Brandt, as well as three submarines, No. 44 in the foreground. 'War' was declared at 4 a.m. and throngs of excited people flocked to see submarines so close to shore. The Barry pilot boat also had an excellent view.

On a return visit to Ilfracombe in August 1904, the crew of HMS *Spartan* landed their gun at the harbour in readiness for a programme of sports at Hillsborough Park. There was a field gun drill and competitions included a wheelbarrow race, a tug of war won by the stokers and a donkey race for officers only.

Storms have often caused great damage and flooding to the harbour and seafront areas. These locals are surveying the damage after a heavy westerly gale on Thursday 12 January 1899, when the sea broke over the Ilfracombe Hotel esplanade wall with tremendous force and wrecked the roof of the swimming baths, smashing 105 panes of glass.

Hurricane-force winds on Monday 4 March 1912, together with a high tide, caused havoc at the eastern end of the Capstone Parade. A thirty-foot breach was made in the wall and the walkway at the base of Capstone was washed away. A contractor who had been working on the path lost tools and scaffolding.

Patron : H.M. QUEEN ALEXANDRA.

EGGS WANTED, for week ending December 15th, 1917.

1ᴰ

EGGS WANTED

THE OFFICIAL ORGAN OF THE NATIONAL EGG COLLECTION.

Subscription 6/- per annum. No. 137   154, Fleet Street, London, E.C.   Price 1d.

MISS LEWIS (of Ilfracombe).

This young lady started work last December and has
up to the present collected 514 Eggs and £1 7s. 2d.
in Cash.

Published for The National Egg Collection Committee by F. Carl.

Craigmore on St Brannocks Road was used as a VAD (Voluntary Aid Detachment) Hospital, which was part of the Red Cross. It was opened on 5 August 1916 and provided convalescent care for British sick and wounded, including sufferers from trench foot and shell-shock. It was demobilised on 31 January 1919 just after this photograph was taken.

Miss Ivy Lewis of Ilfracombe, aged fourteen years, appeared on the front page of the official magazine of *The National Egg Collection for the Wounded* in December 1917. She had collected 514 eggs and £1 7s. 2d. At the end of 1917, over thirty-three million eggs had been dispatched to war-wounded in France and to home hospitals such as Craigmore. Each week, lists of local egg collections appeared in the *Ilfracombe Chronicle*.

Ilfracombe, like every other place in the United Kingdom, rejoiced on 8 May 1945 over the 'supreme triumph' of Victory in Europe. Mr Winston Churchill broadcast the news and 'the moment stirred many hearts in silence… and then in the shouting and singing and parading through the streets'. Flags were raised and red, white and blue blazed over the street tea parties.

At the request of His Majesty King George VI, the Sunday following VE Day was to be observed as a day of thanksgiving prayer to which the Chairman of the Urban District Council, Mrs H. Farndell JP, invited everyone. Each Church minister led prayers and the salute was taken by Colonel Ingpen of the Royal Army Pay Corps.

...and so these are all the times to remember at 'Dear Old Ilfracombe by the Sea'.